The Very Best Secrets of the Hungry Monk

A New Cook Book
featuring
Favourite Recipes
from the last
Forty Years at the
Hungry Monk

Edited by Sue and Nigel Mackenzie
With drawings by Graham Jeffery

Hungry Monk Publications
The Old Coach House
Jevington Near Polegate
BN26 5QF

01323 482178

Also in the same series

The Secrets of the Hungry Monk
The Deeper Secrets of the Hungry Monk
The Hungry Monk at Home
The Secret Sauce Book
Cooking with the Hungry Monk
The Hungry Monk at Work
In Heaven with the Hungry Monk
The Temptations of the Hungry Monk

ISBN 978-0-946478-09-5

Introduction

In the summer of 1967 we came down from London to have lunch with Nigel's mother who was staying at Dean's Place Hotel in Alfriston. We were newly married and dying to work together in the country. She observed what an apparently easy life the owners of the hotel had (how wrong she was!) and suggested that maybe it was something we should consider. Although catering was something we knew nothing about and had never for a moment considered as a career, we were somewhat surprisingly instantly excited by the idea.

In those days there was an estate agent in Alfriston and he had just one hotel on his books -The Monks Rest Hotel in Jevington. We went to see it that afternoon. It looked quite charming, covered in roses, filled with antiques and surrounded by swaying wheat fields. We fell in love with it and agreed to buy it from the very aged owners. At the age of 23 we found ourselves the terrified owners of what was to become The Hungry Monk.

We opening in May 1968 supported by a dedicated 19 year old head chef, Ian Dowding, Sue's glamorous sister Jenny and a bevy of beautiful waitresses.

Like many newly married couples we had given a few dinner parties and that was the only sort of catering we had ever done. We decided to do the same at The Monk and try and create the atmosphere of a country house dinner party - lots of log fires, big sofas and candlelight. We offered the sort of relaxed style of food and service that had been around in London bistros for some years but had not yet reached Sussex.

To our great relief the Monk took off like a rocket - we ran advertisements announcing that Sue and her sister were very lonely and asking people to please visit them as they had fridges full of delicious food and wine and no friends! Within a few weeks they were full every night.

Over the years we have had a number of wonderful chefs who have created so many delicious dishes. To record these we have produced a cook book every few years starting with The Secrets of the Hungry Monk in 1971. Now that we have reached our fortieth anniversary it seems a good idea to celebrate by producing this slim volume featuring a collection of our most popular recipes.

The book is dedicated to all our wonderful customers with heartfelt thanks to all our chefs.

Sue and Nigel Mackenzie

First published in March 2008

This book marks the
40th Anniversary of
The Hungry Monk.

All proceeds from the sale of
this book will go towards
Oxfam's work in Darfur

INDEX

SMOKED HADDOCK and BACON CHOWDER

To serve 4

2 small fillets of smoked haddock
1/4pt/150ml white wine
3-4 large potatoes
1/4pt/150ml double cream
1 onion
4 rashers unsmoked back bacon
2 cloves of garlic
2 sprigs of parsley
1pt/600ml milk
a little olive oil
a knob of unsalted butter
salt and freshly ground black pepper

Preparation

Pre-heat the oven to gas mark 4/180c/350f
Skin the fish by running a sharp knife under the flesh away from the body and holding on to the skin tightly.   Peel and cube the potatoes.   Peel and chop the onion.   Grill the bacon. Peel and crush the garlic and chop up the parsley.

Method

Lay the fillets of haddock in a baking dish, cover with half the milk and season. Cover with foil and place in the oven for 15 minutes.   Remove, reserve the liquor and flake the fish.
In a heavy based pan sweat the vegetables in an equal mixture of olive oil and butter for 5 minutes.   Next simply pour the reserved fish liquor over the vegetables, add the white wine and the rest of the milk.   Bring to the boil and allow to simmer for 10 minutes until the potatoes are cooked.   In order to give a nice thick consistency to the soup, crush some of the potato cubes against the side of the pan and stir in to the mixture.
Finally cut the bacon in to fine strips and add to the mixture together with the flaked fish.   Stir in the double cream and parsley.   Season to taste and serve with crusty warm Walnut Bread.

HOT SUSSEX SMOKIE

Without question this was the most popular starter at The Hungry Monk. Little pots filled with a mixture of smoked haddock flaked in to a rich cheese sauce with a crisp Parmesan topping.

To serve 6

1lb/450grms smoked haddock - skinned and filleted
2oz/50grms unsalted butter
2oz/50grms plain flour
4oz/100grms grated cheddar cheese
a glass of white wine
a bay leaf
freshly ground black pepper
grated Parmesan cheese

Preparation

Poach the haddock in 1.5pts/900ml water with the bay leaf. Cool slightly.

Method

Melt the butter in a saucepan and add the flour to form a roux. After 2 or 3 minutes when the flour is fully cooked take lpt/600ml of the stock from the poached haddock and pour in slowly, stirring all the time. Bring to the boil and simmer for 15 minutes stirring occasionally. Add the cheddar cheese, black pepper and wine. Continue to cook until you have achieved a smooth cheese sauce. Flake in the haddock and spoon the mixture in to 6 small ramekins. Sprinkle Parmesan over the top of each.

If you are serving immediately, flash under the grill until the Parmesan goes golden, otherwise bake in a hot oven for 10 minutes.

SQUID STEW with ROUILLE

Fresh squid stewed in a rich creamy sauce accompanied by a dollop of peppery rouille.

To serve 4

THE STEW

1lb/450grms fresh large squid
4oz/100grms onion
4oz/100grms button mushrooms
10oz/275grms tinned tomatoes
including the juice
1 small green pepper
2 cloves of garlic
1/2pt/300ml Béchamel sauce
5fl oz/125ml dry white wine

2fl oz/50ml single cream
2fl oz/50ml olive oil
1 dessertspoon of white wine
vinegar
Herbes de Provence
Dijon mustard
Tabasco sauce
salt

Preparation

The price one pays for the pleasure of eating fresh squid is preparing it. A job that should be done on the draining board of your sink. Start by cutting off all the tentacles by the head and setting to one side. Next grasp the head firmly and pull steadily away from the body. Unless you are very unlucky all the entrails will come too and the whole lot can be thrown away. Remove the spine which appears to be made of clear plastic and wash the body inside and out. Peel off and discard the skin. Cut off the fins and slice in to thin strips. Cut the body in to rings about 1/4in. thick. Finally chop up the two long tentacles.

Peel and slice the onion. De-seed and slice the pepper. Wipe and slice the mushrooms. Peel and crush the garlic with a little salt. Chop the tinned tomatoes and reserve the juice.

Method

Take a saucepan large enough to accommodate all the ingredients and commence by cooking the onion, pepper, mushrooms, garlic and a large pinch of Herbes de Provence in the olive oil until they are soft. Add the squid and cook until it becomes opaque. Now tip in the tomatoes, white wine, a teaspoon of mustard, the wine vinegar, 2 shakes of tabasco and a pinch of salt. Bring to the boil, add the Béchamel sauce and cook gently for 30 minutes. Finish by stirring in the cream and adjust the seasoning.

THE ROUILLE

1 x 7oz/200grms tin of red pimentos
1.5oz/40grms stale white bread
without the crusts
2 tablespoons of olive oil

the juice of 1/4 of a lemon
2 cloves of garlic
1/4 of a level teaspoon of cayenne
salt

Method

Drain the pimentos. Gently fry the garlic in the oil until soft but not coloured. Now tip all the ingredients in to a liquidiser and pulverise to a thick puree.

To serve

Nothing could be simpler. Just heat the stew, ladle in to fairly deep bowls and hand round the rouille and slices of crusty French bread.

FISHCAKES with RED PEPPER and SHERRY SAUCE

To serve 4
1lb/450grms maris piper potatoes
4oz/100grms salted butter
2 shallots
8oz/225grs smoked haddock fillets
8oz/225grms sea bass fillets
8oz/225grms salmon fillets
a bay leaf
a tablespoon dill
a tablespoon chives
a tablespoon of parsley
grated zest of 2 lemons
4oz/100grms plain flour
2 eggs
6oz/175grms brown breadcrumbs
salt and freshly ground black pepper
vegetable oil

THE SAUCE
3 red peppers
1 red onion
1/2pt/300ml white wine
2.5fl oz/75ml dry sherry
1/4pt/150ml double cream
salt and black pepper

Preparation
Peel, boil and mash the potatoes with half the butter.   Season with salt and pepper.   Peel and finely chop 2 of the shallots and saute them in the rest of the butter until soft but not coloured.   Poach the fish with the bay leaf in enough water to cover.   Bring to the boil and then put a lid on the pan and remove from the heat.
Pre-heat the oven to gas mark 5/190c/375f.

Method
Once cool enough to handle, remove the fish from its liquor.   Remove any skin and flake the fish in to the mashed potato, with the shallots, herbs and lemon zest.
Shape in to 4 large or 8 small cakes.   Dip in to plain flour, beaten egg and then the breadcrumbs before setting aside on a baking tray in the fridge to chill for at least 30 minutes.

The Sauce
Finely chop and de-seed the peppers.   Peel and finely chop the onion.   Take a heavy based pan and gently cook the peppers and onion in the wine with the lid on until soft.   Puree in a liquidiser and then pass the mixture through a sieve in to a clean saucepan.
Heat some oil in a pan and fry the fishcakes for 3 - 4 minutes on each side until crisp and golden.   Transfer to the preheated oven to heat through for 10 minutes.
Gently bring the sauce to the boil and whisk in the cream and sherry.   Serve the fishcakes surrounded by the sauce.

PRAWN, CRAB and SMOKED SALMON ROULADE

A fish soufflé roulade filled with prawns, crab and smoked salmon

To serve 10-12

ROULADE BASE

1lb/450grms plaice or lemon sole - filleted and skinned
4 eggs
1/4pt/150ml double cream
grated nutmeg
salt and black pepper

10oz/250grms white crabmeat (well drained if using frozen)
4oz/100grms sliced smoked salmon
1 tablespoonful of chopped parsley
1 tablespoonful of chopped canned pimentos
1/2pt/300ml thick Mayonnaise

FILLING

10oz/250grms peeled prawns (well drained if using frozen)

Equipment A shallow baking tray 16in. x 12in.

Preparation

Pre-heat the oven to gas mark 8/230c/450f. Separate the eggs. Cut a piece of greaseproof paper that is large enough to exactly cover the base and side of the baking tray. As you need to oil both sides of this paper the best way is to brush the tray itself with oil and then press first one side of the paper in to place, lift it off, turn it over and press the other side down.

Method

Firstly poach the fish in some salted water, drain well and allow to cool. Transfer the fish to a liquidiser and puree with the egg yolks, nutmeg and seasoning. Whip the egg whites in a large bowl until stiff, fold in the fish puree and the cream.   The mixture is now ready to be poured on to the greaseproof paper and spread with a palette knife to an even thickness from corner to corner. Place on the top shelf of the oven to cook for 10-15 minutes until golden. Allow to cool.

The Filling

Mix the prawns, crabmeat, pimentos and parsley in to the mayonnaise.

Assembly

The idea is to end up with something that looks like a Swiss roll.   Firstly remove the greaseproof paper by gently placing the base face down on a fresh piece of paper and easing off the greaseproof, starting at the corners and side edges.   Great care must be taken here as it is only too easy to tear the base which will make rolling up with the filling inside very difficult.

The next task is to cover the base first with slices of smoked salmon and then evenly spread over the fish and mayonnaise mixture.   Because the whole thing is about to be rolled it makes life very much easier if the mixture is not spread down a 1in. border at the beginning of the roll and again at the end.

Now starting with the uncovered border furthest away from you, gently roll the base up towards you using the greaseproof paper to give even support. Allow the roulade to stand in the fridge for about 2hrs. covered in cling film.

When you are ready to serve, carve in to thick slices.   The roulade is at its best the day that it is made.

" Which brings me, dear friends, to my final point "

THE MIDNIGHT SNACK

A glorious concoction of seafood thickly spread on rye bread

To serve 6

3/4pt/450ml **thick mayonnaise**
6oz/150grms **peeled cooked prawns**
6oz/150grms **white crabmeat**
1oz/25grms **anchovies**
2 **rollmops**
1 **teaspoon curry powder**
1 **red onion**
2 **cloves of garlic**
the juice of half a lemon
tabasco
freshly ground black pepper
6 **slices of whole grain rye bread**

Preparation

Drain and finely chop the rollmops.   Drain and pound the anchovies.   Peel and crush the garlic with a little salt.   Peel and finely chop the onion.

Method

Mix the anchovies, garlic, curry powder, lemon juice and onion in to the mayonnaise.   Tip in the rollmops, drained prawns and crabmeat.   Stir well and adjust the seasoning with a few shakes of tabasco, salt and black pepper.
Dollop on to the slices of rye bread and serve with a little watercress salad.

CREAMY SQUID and PRAWN RISOTTO

To serve 4

3 medium squid
8 tiger prawns
8oz/200grms arborio risotto rice
2 shallots
5oz/125grms unsalted butter
2 tablespoons of olive oil
1.5pt/900ml vegetable stock

3fl oz/90ml dry white vermouth
4oz/100grms grated Parmesan
2fl oz/60ml double cream
the juice of a lemon
salt and black pepper
2 tablespoons of chopped parsley
fresh Parmesan shards

Preparation

Peel and chop the shallots. Prepare the squid by cleaning them, taking off any skin and slicing them in to thin strips. Shell the prawns. Stir the vermouth in to the stock.

Method

Take a large heavy based pan and combine the butter and the oil over a gentle heat. Once hot, tip in the onion and sweat until soft but not coloured. Pour in the rice and cook for one minute. Now, stirring gradually, add the stock and vermouth a ladleful at a time until all has been absorbed by the rice. This is a time consuming process but resist the temptation to pour in all the stock and walk away as this will result in a pudding-like lump of rice which is not what we want.

Now stir the squid and prawns in to the risotto, followed by the lemon juice, parsley, cream and grated Parmesan. Season to taste and serve in warmed bowls with shards of Parmesan on top.

FARMHOUSE TERRINE

To serve 8-12
8oz/200grms duck and/or chicken livers
8oz/200grms minced raw pork liver
8oz/200grms minced raw pork
4oz/100grms minced raw ham
14-16 rashers of rindless streaky bacon
2oz/50grms salted butter
1 onion
3 cloves of garlic
a large tot of brandy
a wine glass of strong red wine
12 button mushrooms
2 bay leaves
Herbes de Provence
olive oil
1 egg
1/2pt/300ml double cream
fresh ground black pepper

EQUIPMENT
1 cast iron terrine dish 12in x 3in

Preparation
Pre-heat the oven to gas mark 3/170c/325f.
Roughly chop the duck and/or chicken livers. Peel and chop the onion. Peel and crush the garlic with a little salt. Beat the egg in to the cream. Lightly grease the terrine dish with oil. Line with greaseproof paper, put the two bay leaves in the bottom and then arrange the overlapping slices of bacon, making sure to have enough bacon and greaseproof left over to envelop the whole terrine once it is filled.

Method
Melt the butter and over a fierce heat fry the onion, herbs and garlic. Pour in the brandy and set alight. When the flames have died down stir in the red wine.
Add the rest of the ingredients except the cream and the egg. Cook gently for 10 minutes. Take off the heat and stir in the egg and cream mixture.
Season with black pepper. Pour the whole mixture in to the previously lined terrine dish folding over the overhanging strips of bacon and greaseproof.
Cover the top of the dish with tin foil and place in a roasting tray half filled with water. Cook in the pre-heated oven for 60-80minutes. Allow to cool slightly before placing in the fridge overnight with heavy weights on top to compress the terrine.
When ready to serve, turn out the terrine and serve in slices with hot toast.

DUCK and POTATO CAKE with APPLE and SAGE SAUCE

This is the ducky brother of fishcakes - we call them *Quakes*!

To serve 4

4 duck legs
6oz/150grms new potatoes
3 medium old potatoes
2 tablespoons of double cream
4 spring onions
2 egg yolks
salt and fresh ground black pepper
6oz/175grms fresh breadcrumbs
4 oz/100grms plain flour
2 eggs
vegetable oil

FOR THE SAUCE
6 apples
1/4pt/150ml cider
2oz/50grms sugar
3fl oz/90ml single cream
6 sage leaves

Preparation
Pre-heat the oven to gas mark 5/190c/375f.   Season the duck legs and roast them for about an hour in the pre-heated oven.   Whilst they are roasting boil and dice the new potatoes.   Peel, boil and mash the old potatoes with the cream and season with salt and black pepper.   Trim and chop the spring onions   Peel and chop the apples and chop the sage leaves for the sauce.

Method
You will have time to make the sauce whilst the duck legs are roasting.
In a heavy based pan simply cook the apples, cider and sugar until soft.
Remove from the heat and puree in a food processor.   Return to the heat, stir in the cream and sage.   Season to taste.

Now the duck cakes.   Take the meat off the duck legs and roughly chop.
Put in to a large bowl and tip in the new potatoes, mashed potatoes, spring onions and egg yolks.   Thoroughly mix all this before adjusting the seasoning.   Now shape the mixture in to something resembling a fishcake.
You can either make 4 large or 8 small ones.   Dip in to plain flour, beaten egg and then the breadcrumbs before setting aside on a baking tray in the fridge to chill for at least 30 minutes.

When you are ready to serve them, heat some oil in a pan and fry them for 3 or 4 minutes on each side until crisp, golden and utterly appetising to look at.
Transfer them to the oven to heat through for 10 minutes.   Serve with the Apple and Sage sauce.

POACHED EGG and PEA PUREE TART with HOLLANDAISE

A crisp individual tart filled with pea puree and a freshly poached egg topped with Hollandaise

To serve 4

shortcrust pastry
1lb/450grms petit pois
3.5fl oz/100ml double cream
salt and freshly ground black pepper
8 eggs
white wine vinegar
1/2pt/300ml Hollandaise sauce

EQUIPMENT
4 x 4in diameter - 1in deep
loose bottomed flan tins

Preparation

There are four tasks to be performed for this dish - make the pea puree, make the tarts, make the Hollandaise sauce and poach the eggs. Leave the poaching of the eggs until last.

Method

Make 4 shortcrust pastry tarts, baking blind in the usual way. If you need help with these see page 101 of In Heaven with The Hungry Monk.

Boil the petit pois until soft, drain and whizz them in a food processor with the cream, salt and pepper. Now puree the mixture through a sieve .

Make the Hollandaise sauce in the usual way and keep warm at kitchen temperature - the recipe for this can be found on page 104 of In Heaven with The Hungry Monk.

Now the eggs need to be poached. At the risk of offending experienced cooks, just a word of advice on poaching these. Pour water in to a saucepan to a level of 3in. deep. Add a few drops of white wine vinegar - no salt as this makes the whites go rubbery - bring to a rolling boil and crack the eggs in to a teacup one at a time. Slip these gently in to the boiling water and poach for about 3 minutes, taking care not to overcook them as we want the yokes to remain runny.

To assemble the dish, make sure all the ingredients are warm and then spoon the puree in to each tart, position a poached egg on top and then cover with Hollandaise

main courses

PAN FRIED FILLET of SALMON with GREEN CHILLI and YELLOW PEPPER RISOTTO

To serve 4

4 x 6oz/150grms fillets of best Scotch salmon
3oz/75grms unsalted butter
2 tablespoons olive oil
4oz/100grms arborio risotto rice
half an onion
3/4pt/400ml vegetable stock
2 green chillies
1 yellow pepper
salt and freshly ground black pepper

Preparation
Peel and finely chop the onion.   Chop the chillies and yellow pepper.

Method
Sweat the pepper, chillies and onion in half the butter and a tablespoon of oil until soft but not coloured.   Add more butter and the arborio rice.   Slowly add some of the vegetable stock, a little at a time, stirring as you go.   Do not season at this stage.   You will want to cook the rice for about 30 minutes until just soft to the taste.   The risotto is now ready and you should season it to taste.

Pan fry the fillets of salmon in a little butter and oil, salt and pepper for about 3-5 minutes on each side.

Serve each fillet on the risotto.

SALMON and HALIBUT en CROUTE

Salmon layered with halibut, Danish caviar and prawns and baked in puff pastry

To serve 8

1 x 2lb/1kilo piece of fresh Scotch salmon
1lb/450grms fresh halibut - skinned and filleted
4oz/100grms prawns - cooked and peeled
2oz/50grms Danish lump fish roe
4oz/100grms salted butter
1lb/450grms uncooked puff pastry
salt and freshly ground black pepper
1 egg
half a cup of milk
poppy seeds
Hollandaise sauce

Preparation

Cut the salmon away from the bone until it is possible to completely remove all the bone. This should leave the fish in two equally sized pieces. Remove the skin. Beat the egg and milk together to form an egg wash.

Method

Lay one piece of the salmon flat on the table. Spread the upper surface with half the butter and black pepper followed by the lump fish roe. Next place the fillet of halibut on top and trim to size. Follow this with the rest of the butter, more black pepper and prawns and top with the remaining half of salmon. Press firmly together.
Now roll out a piece of pastry large enough to completely envelop the fish with adequate margin for overlap. Clamp all the edges together sealing with egg wash. Using the remaining egg wash, brush the top surface of the pastry and sprinkle with poppy seeds. Make a few steam vents with a sharp knife. Place on a baking tray in the fridge and allow to stand for 1 hour.

Pre-heat the oven to gas mark 8/230c/450f.
Bake in the centre of the oven for 20-25 minutes until thoroughly cooked - the pastry will be deep brown. Allow to rest in a warm place for 5 minutes before serving in thick slices with Hollandaise sauce.

This is also delicious served cold with salad and mayonnaise.

SEAFOOD PANCAKES

Very thin savoury pancakes filled with prawns, sole, lobster and scallops in a creamy white wine sauce.

To serve 6

1lb/450grms sole, skinned and filleted
1.5lb/675grms lobster to produce
10oz/225grms meat
6oz/150grms prawns
10 medium sized scallops
a large tot of brandy
a glass of dry white wine
water
a bay leaf

the juice of 2 lemons
salt and black pepper
4oz/100grms salted butter
4 shallots
4oz/100grms plain flour
1/4pt/150ml single cream
grated Parmesan cheese
12 pancakes

Preparation
Cook the lobster. Remove the meat from the shell and chop in to large chunks. Poach the sole and scallops in the wine, adding water to cover, with the bay leaf, lemon juice and seasoning. Reserve this stock. Peel and finely chop the shallots. Pre-heat the oven to gas mark 6/200c/400f.

Method
To make the sauce - melt the butter in a pan and fry the shallots until soft but not coloured. Stir in the flour and cook for a minute or two before adding 2 pints/1 litre of the reserved fish stock. Bring to the boil, stirring from time to time and then simmer for 15 minutes. Remove from the heat, cool slightly before stirring in the cream. Adjust the seasoning.

Take the sole and the scallops and chop in to small chunks. Tip in to a bowl and add the prawns and the lobster meat. Heat the brandy in a small saucepan and set alight. Before the flames die down quickly pour it over the fish. Pour half the sauce over the fish and reserve the rest.

Assembly
Half an hour before eating the dish divide the seafood mixture between the 12 pancakes. Roll them up tightly and lay in a buttered shallow fireproof dish. Spoon over the rest of the sauce and sprinkle with Parmesan. Place in the pre-heated oven for 10 minutes or until heated through.

STUFFED RABBIT with MUSTARD SAUCE

This dish has been a stalwart favourite at The Hungry Monk. We have varied the stuffing according to the seasons. This one is with a couscous and pistachio stuffing.

To serve 4

4 x boned rabbit thighs
4 rabbit fillets
6oz/150grms couscous
4oz/100grms pistachio nuts
3oz/75grms sausage meat
4 sheets prosciutto ham
4 leaves of sorrel
salt and black pepper
small bunch of flat leaf parsley
salt and freshly ground black pepper

THE SAUCE
1/2pt/300ml chicken stock
1/4pt/150ml double cream
a glass of dry white wine
2 glasses of madeira
1 dessertspoon Dijon mustard
1 dessertspoon whole grain
mustard

Preparation

Pre-heat the oven to gas mark 6/200c/400f
Prepare the couscous by covering in near boiling water for 10 - 15 minutes. Stir in a little olive oil as this prevents it from sticking together. Finely chop the pistachio nuts. Chop the sorrel and parsley.

Method

Mix the couscous, sausage meat, pistachio nuts, sorrel and a little of the parsley in to a paste. Put an equal amount inside each rabbit thigh and wrap around each with a sheet of prosciutto. There should be no need to secure this but if you want to you can use a cocktail stick and remember to remove it after the cooking.
Place the thighs on a greased baking tray and cook in the centre of the pre-heated oven for 20 - 30 minutes. After 15 minutes of cooking put the fillets in to the oven with a little olive oil. Do not overcook these.

MUSTARD SAUCE

In a heavy based pan combine the chicken stock and mustard with the madeira and white wine. Bring to the boil and reduce by approximately half. Finish by stirring in the cream and adjust the seasoning.

BREAST of GUINEA FOWL stuffed with BLACK PUDDING and APPLE with MADEIRA SAUCE

To serve 4
4 breasts of guinea fowl
2 eating apples
2 shallots
1lb/450grms black pudding
4 springs of fresh thyme
a clove of garlic
olive oil
a knob of unsalted butter
salt and freshly ground black pepper

FOR THE SAUCE
1pt/600ml madeira
3/4pt/450ml chicken stock
salt and ground black pepper

Preparation
Peel and finely chop the apples and shallots. Peel and crush the garlic with a little salt. In a saute pan melt the butter with the oil and soften the shallots and apples. Stir in the black pudding, garlic and thyme. Season. Make a pocket between the skin of the guinea fowl and the flesh and stuff a quarter of the mixture in to each breast. Set aside in the fridge for 30 minutes.

Method
Pre-heat the oven to gas mark 4/180c/350f. Take a roasting tin and brush it with olive oil. Season the guinea fowl on both sides, place them in the tin and drizzle over some more olive oil. Roast in the oven for 20 to 25 minutes until cooked.

Meanwhile combine the madeira and stock in a heavy based shallow pan and reduce until syrupy. Season to taste and serve alongside the guinea fowl. This sauce is quite intense so you only need a little.

Accompany with creamy parmesan mash or gratin dauphinoise and braised red cabbage.

PARTRIDGE with CABBAGE

To serve 2

2 partridges
Half a Dutch white cabbage
Half a Spanish onion
1/2pt/300ml jellied chicken stock
a glass of dry white wine
4oz/100grms rindless streaky bacon
a small handful of sultanas
4oz/100grms unsalted butter
Herbes de Provence
salt and freshly ground black pepper

Preparation
Pre-heat the oven to gas mark 3/170c/325f.
Split the birds in half lengthways removing the spine and ribs.   Peel and slice
the onion.   Shred the cabbage.   Cut the bacon in to lardons.

Method
Bring a pan of salted water to the boil and blanche the cabbage.   Drain and
set aside.   Melt the butter in a shallow pan and saute the onion and bacon
until soft.   Mix in to the cabbage with the sultanas.   Using the same saute
pan, brown the partridges on all sides, seasoning with salt, pepper and
herbes de Provence.   Lift out and keep warm.   Pour the wine in to the pan
juices and reduce by half before stirring in the stock .

Assembly
Take a buttered casserole.   The idea is to layer the cabbage and partridges,
seasoning as you go and ending with a layer of cabbage.   Now pour in the
stock.   Close the lid on the casserole using dampened greaseproof paper to
ensure a good seal.   Cook for between 1 and 2 hours until the partridges are
tender.   Serve with creamy mashed potato and sautéed field mushrooms.

BREAST of CORN FED CHICKEN with PESTO SAUCE and SWEETCORN MASH

To serve 4
4 x corn fed chicken breasts with skin
olive oil
salt and freshly ground black pepper
unsalted butter

THE MASH
2lbs/900grms maris piper potatoes
9oz/225grms tinned sweetcorn
2oz/50grms unsalted butter
2 tablespoons single cream
1 tablespoon of milk
salt and freshly ground black pepper

THE SAUCE
2oz/50grms fresh basil
6fl oz/175ml olive oil
a tablespoon balsamic vinegar
the juice of a lemon
a dessertspoon Dijon mustard
2 cloves garlic - peeled
1oz/25grms roasted pine nuts
salt and black pepper

Preparation
Pre-heat the oven to gas mark 5/190c/375f
Make the sauce by whizzing together all the ingredients except the olive oil and pine nuts in a food processor.   Pour on the olive oil in a gentle stream and adjust the thickness if necessary by either adding more olive oil or more lemon juice.   Set aside.
Peel and slice the potatoes.   Keep in cold water.

Method
Take a heavy based frying pan and heat the olive oil with the butter until foaming. Season the chicken breasts and fry them skin side down for 2 or 3 minutes until sealed and golden.   Turn over and seal the other side.
Transfer to a roasting tin and cook them in the preheated oven for about 20 minutes until the juices run clear.

Whilst they are roasting you can make the sweetcorn mash. Boil the peeled and sliced potatoes until soft.   Drain and mash with butter and cream.   Heat the sweetcorn in a little water and then drain.   Puree a third of it with a tablespoon of milk.   Stir this puree in to the mashed potato followed by the rest of the sweetcorn. Taste, season and keep warm.

To serve
Gently warm the pesto sauce, toss in the roasted pine nuts and adjust the seasoning.
Pile potato and sweetcorn mash on to warm plates, rest the chicken breast on top and drizzle the pesto sauce over half the chicken and around the plate.

CASSOULET of PORK and DUCK

Wonderfully tasty and filling peasant food. Ideal after a hard day in the fields washed down with plenty of rough red wine

To serve 6 - 8
6 duck breasts
1lb/450grms dried haricot beans
2lbs/900grms belly of pork
12 small Toulouse sausages
12 rashers of rindless streaky bacon
12 tomatoes
2 large onions
2pts/1.2 litres chicken stock
3/4pt/450ml strong red wine
6 tablespoons fresh breadcrumbs mixed with
3 tablespoons grated Parmesan cheese
3 - 4 cloves garlic
3 pinches of Herbes de Provence
salt and freshly ground black pepper

Preparation
Soak the beans in cold water overnight. Slice the pork and bacon in to lardons. Peel and roughly chop the onions. Peel and crush the garlic with a little salt. Peel, de-seed and roughly chop the tomatoes. Pre-heat the oven to gas mark 4/180c/350f.

Method
Drain the beans and stew in a large heavy based pan with 1 pint of the stock for up to an hour until the beans are tender. In a separate pan fry the duck breasts in a little olive oil, skin side down, over a low heat until the skin is crisp. Remove from the heat. Lift out the breasts, retaining a cupful of the duck fat, and allow to cool. Gently remove the skin which will be used later and chop the duck meat in to slices one inch thick.

We can now commence the preparation of the Cassoulet itself by taking a large ovenproof pot and frying, in the duck fat, the garlic, onions, bacon, pork, sausages and Herbes de Provence until brown. Next pour in the remaining stock, red wine, tomatoes and tomato puree and reduce by a third. Finally tip in the beans and the duck meat, stir thoroughly and season.

Cover the pot and transfer to the middle of the oven to cook for about an hour and a half until thick but not dry.

Remove the lid, arrange the duck skin over the top and finish by liberally sprinkling over the breadcrumb and parmesan mixture. Brown under the grill and serve with bunches of watercress.

CRISP BREAST of DUCK with SPICED PLUM and BALSAMIC SAUCE

To serve 4
2 large ducks with the legs removed
3 eating apples
sprigs of fresh sage
salt

THE SAUCE

6 plums
1/2pt/300ml red wine
4fl oz/100ml balsamic vinegar
2oz/50grms sugar
1 cinnamon stick
4 cloves
4 cardamom pods
2 bay leaves

1/4pt/150ml chicken stock
2 tablespoons orange juice
2.5fl oz/75ml red wine
salt and ground black pepper
2oz/50grms butter

Preparation

Start by quartering and stoning the plums.   Then in a heavy based pan combine the red wine, balsamic vinegar, sugar, cinnamon, cloves, cardamon pods and bay leaves and cook until reduced by half.   Remove from the heat and tip in the plums. Allow this mixture to stand for about an hour to give the plums a chance to absorb the spices.

Pre-heat the oven to gas mark 6/200c/400f.   Prick the skin of the duck breasts all over with a sharp fork to release the fat from under the skin during cooking.   Rub well with salt to help the skin go really crisp.   Place upside down in a roasting tray with no fat and set in the upper part of the oven to cook for 40 minutes to 1 hour.   At the end of this time the ducks should be cooked but not yet crisp.

Allow to cool for 30 minutes and then break the carcasses in half to give you four separate breasts.   Trim these so that they will look neat on the plate. Now lay the breasts, skin side up, on a bed of sliced apples and fresh sage in a roasting tin and return them to the oven to cook for a further 15 to 20 minutes until crisp.

Turning back to the plum sauce - separate the plums from their liquor and put them to one side.   Add the stock, orange juice and remaining red wine to the plum liquor and pass it through a strainer.   Return the liquor to the heat and reduce by about half until syrupy.

When you are ready to serve, transfer the sauce to a clean saucepan, heat through and whisk in the butter to make it shiny, then add the plums and heat through.   Serve the duck breasts surrounded by the sauce.   Do not pour the sauce over the duck otherwise the crisp skin will go soggy.

BEST END of LAMB with PORT, REDCURRANT and ORANGE SAUCE

A delicious combination of the most tender part of the lamb and a crisp savoury coating served with a sharp fruity sauce

To serve 2

THE LAMB
1 best end of English Lamb
2oz/50grms fresh breadcrumbs
a clove of garlic
2 anchovy fillets

THE SAUCE
a wine glass of port
2 oranges
2 tablespoons of redcurrant jelly
a sprig of rosemary and thyme
seasoned plain flour
1 egg
a little milk

Preparation

Combine the breadcrumbs with the herbs, peeled garlic and anchovies in a food processor. Trim the excess fat from the lamb. Beat the egg and milk together to form an egg wash. Carefully peel the zest from the oranges and shred it finely. Remove the pith from the oranges and fillet the segments. Pre-heat the oven to gas mark 6/200c/400f.

Method

Firstly take the lamb and placing it on the table bones down, sprinkle the entire joint with flour. Follow this with a good thick coating of egg wash. Pat the breadcrumb and anchovy mixture on to the sticky egg washed surface of the lamb and place on a roasting tray in the oven for 30 - 45 minutes depending on the size of the joint and how pink you like your lamb.

The sauce is simply made. In a small saucepan combine the redcurrant jelly, port, orange zest and segments. Cook gently until hot.

To serve, either cut the best end in half and hand the sauce separately or slice in to individual chops.

FILLET of BEEF WELLINGTON

By no means unique to The Hungry Monk but undoubtedly one of our favourite ways of cooking fillet steak

To serve 8

1 x 4lb/2 kilos fillet of prime Scotch beef
2oz/50grms salted butter
24 field mushrooms
12 rashers of unsmoked rindless streaky bacon
1.5lbs/675grms uncooked puff pastry
1 egg
half a cup of milk
freshly ground black pepper

Preparation

Trim the fat and sinew off the fillet.   Saute the mushrooms in butter until soft.   Beat the egg and milk together to form an egg wash.   Pre-heat the oven to gas mark 7/220c/425f.

Method

Firstly fold the pointed end of the fillet under the middle so that the fillet has approximately the same girth throughout.   Sprinkle liberally with black pepper.
Roll out the puff pastry to a square sufficient to encase the entire fillet. Position the fillet in the centre of the pastry and wrap it on all sides with the bacon and mushrooms.   Dampen all four edges of the pastry - wrap and seal.   Brush with egg wash and roast in the over for 45 minutes to 1 hour depending on how rare you like your beef.   Remove from the oven and rest in a warm place for 10 minutes before carving in to thick slices.

You can substitute chicken liver pate for the bacon and mushrooms if you feel like a change.

puddings

IT'S JUST HEAVEN

THE ORIGINAL HUNGRY MONK BANOFFI PIE

Sliced bananas and whipped cream over a thick layer of soft toffee. It is ironic that of the many sophisticated dishes we have created over the years, this simple pudding invented thirty-five years ago and temporarily named Banoffi Pie has become one of the most popular puddings in the world.

To serve 8-10

12oz/300grms uncooked shortcrust pastry
1.5 tins condensed milk (1lb 5oz/600grms)
1.5lbs/700grms firm bananas
1pt/600ml double cream
a level teaspoon of powdered instant coffee
a dessertspoon of caster sugar
a little freshly ground coffee

Preparation

Make a shortcrust pastry flan case and bake blind. Allow to cool.

The secret of this delicious pudding lies in the condensed milk. Immerse the cans *unopened* in a deep pan of boiling water. Cover and boil for 3 hours making sure that the pan does not boil dry - *see caution below*. Remove the tins from the water and allow to cool completely before opening. Inside you will now find the soft toffee filling.

Method

Whip the cream with the instant coffee and sugar until thick and smooth. Now spread the toffee over the base of the flan. Peel and then halve the bananas lengthways and lay them on the toffee. Finally, spoon or pipe on the cream and lightly sprinkle over the fresh ground coffee.

CAUTION

It is absolutely vital to top up the pan of boiling water frequently during the cooking of the cans - 3 hours is a long time. If they are allowed to boil dry, the cans will explode causing a grave risk to life, limb and kitchen ceilings.

Hint

Banoffi is a marvellous 'emergency' pudding once you have the toffee mixture in your store cupboard. We therefore suggest that you boil several extra cans at the same time, as they will keep unopened indefinitely.

TREACLE PUDDING with ORANGE CUSTARD

To serve 6
3oz/75grms plain flour
3oz/75grms self-raising flour
2oz/50grms caster sugar
1 level teaspoon baking powder
1 egg
1/4pt/150ml milk
3oz/75grms suet
1lb/450grms golden syrup
the grated zest of a lemon

Equipment   6 x 1/4pt/150ml pudding basins with lids or greaseproof paper and tin foil tied on with string

Method
This is a delightfully simple pudding and need not be heavy and stodgy.
Mix the egg and milk together.   Place all the ingredients except for the golden syrup, egg and milk in to a mixing bowl.   Stir together and make a well in the centre.   Pour in the egg and milk mixture and gradually incorporate all the dry ingredients until you have a smooth batter.

Now pour golden syrup in to the bottom of each pudding basin to a depth of 3/4 inch and top up with the batter.   Seal tightly and cook for 40 - 45 minutes in a steamer.   Turn out upside down and serve warm with:-

HOME-MADE ORANGE CUSTARD

6 egg yolks
3/4pt/450ml milk
3oz/75grms caster sugar
the zest of an orange
a vanilla pod

Method
Mix the sugar and egg yolks together in a bowl.   Heat the milk with the vanilla pod and orange zest.   Bring gently to the boil and immediately remove from the heat and allow to stand for a few minutes so that the flavours infuse.   Lift out the vanilla pod and pour the milk on to the egg yolks and sugar, stirring with a wooden spoon.   Return the custard to the pan and heat gently, stirring all the time, until the custard will coat the back of the spoon.   It is now ready to serve with the Treacle Puddings.

EXCEPTIONAL CHOCOLATE PUDDING

We make these individually. They are deliciously spongy on top and gooey underneath

To serve 6
2oz/50grms unsalted butter
4oz/100grms dark brown sugar
2 eggs
1.5oz/40grms self-raising flour
2 tablespoons cocoa powder
12fl oz/350ml milk
2 tablespoons cocoa powder
a knob of unsalted butter

EQUIPMENT
6 x 2.5in diameter deep ramekins

Preparation
Pre-heat the oven to gas mark 4/180c/350f
Butter the ramekins and separate the eggs. Combine the milk and 2 tablespoons of cocoa and heat until you have made chocolate milk. Set aside to cool.

Method
Take a large bowl and beat the butter and sugar until pale and fluffy. Beat in the egg yolks. Sift in the flour and remaining 2 tablespoons of cocoa powder. Then stir in the chocolate milk. In a separate bowl whisk the egg whites until stiff and fold into the chocolate mixture. Pour in to the waiting ramekins. Place them in a roasting tin half filled with hot water. Cover with foil and bake in the oven for 30 minutes.

ATHOL BROSE

For those who love a drop of the hard stuff in their pud

To serve 6
1pt/600ml double cream
4 tablespoons of thin clear honey
a large tot of whisky

Method
The great beauty of this pudding is its simplicity. Just whisk all the ingredients together until you have a thick creamy consistency.

Serve in 6 pretty glasses with Almond Tuiles.

WARM MADEIRA CAKE with BUTTERSCOTCH SAUCE

To serve 6-8

THE CAKE
6oz/150grms unsalted butter
6oz/150grms caster sugar
3 eggs
6oz/150grms self-raising flour

THE SAUCE
1lb/450grms golden syrup
4oz/100grms unsalted butter

Equipment
1 cake tin 7in. diameter x 3in. deep

Preparation
Pre-heat the oven to gas mark 3/170c/325f
Grease the cake tin

Method
Beat the butter and sugar together until pale and creamy.   Beat in the eggs and fold in the sifted flour.   Spoon the mixture in to the cake tin and bake in the middle of the oven for 75 - 90 minutes until firm to the touch.   Cool slightly and then turn out on to a wire rack.

To make the sauce, gently heat the golden syrup and butter together in a heavy based pan, stirring from time to time, until you have a smooth thick sauce. It should be served hot but not boiling.

As this cake should be eaten warm, the ideal is to serve it straight away with vanilla ice cream and butterscotch sauce.   However if you are making it in advance you can always heat it up later by giving it a quick blast in the microwave or wrap it up in tin foil and put in to a hot oven for 5-8 minutes.

CREAMY RICE PUDDING BRULEE with APRICOT and COINTREAU COMPOTE

To serve 4

THE RICE PUDDING
3oz/75grms short grain rice
1/2pt/300ml water
1/2pt/300ml milk
1oz/25grms caster sugar
2 egg yolks
2.5fl oz/75ml double cream
a knob of unsalted butter
icing sugar for dusting

THE COMPOTE
8 fresh or dried apricots
1/4pt/150ml water
1 tablespoon caster sugar
2 tablespoons cointreau

EQUIPMENT
6 x dariole moulds

Preparation
Pre-heat the oven to gas mark 4/180c/350f.   Butter the dariole moulds.
In a heavy based pan cover the rice with the cold water, bring to the boil and
simmer for 10 minutes.   Drain, refresh under the cold tap and drain again.
This process removes the starch from the rice.

Apricot Compote
Stone and slice the apricots and combine in a heavy based pan with the
water, sugar and cointreau.   Stew gently until the apricots are soft but not
broken up.   Remove from the heat and set aside.

Method
In a heavy based pan bring three quarters of the milk, half the sugar and all
the butter to the boil.   Tip in the rice and simmer for 8-10 minutes.   Remove
from the heat.   Take a large china bowl and beat the yolks with the remaining
sugar.

In a separate pan bring the cream with the rest of the milk to the boil.   Pour
this straight on to the egg and sugar mixture whisking continuously to form
a smooth custard.   Now pour the custard in to the rice mixture and return to
a low heat to thicken slightly.   Pour this rice mixture in to the buttered dariole
moulds and place in a deep roasting tin half filled with hot water.   Cover with
a large sheet of foil and bake in the oven for 20 - 30 minutes until set.
Remove from the oven and allow to cool.   Chill in the fridge for at least
2 hours.

To serve
Turn the puddings out of the moulds with the help of a sharp knife.   Sprinkle
with icing sugar and brulee under a hot grill or with the help of a kitchen blow
torch.   Serve immediately with the Apricot Compote.

CHOCOLATE PANNA COTTA

To serve 16

1pt/600ml double cream
5fl oz/150ml milk
5oz/120grms caster sugar
9oz/250grms dark chocolate
2 tablespoons rum
3 sheets of leaf gelatine

Method
Soak the gelatine in cold water until soft.   Break the chocolate in to pieces and melt in a bowl over simmering hot water.   In a heavy based pan bring the milk and cream gently to the boil.   Remove from the heat and whisk in the sugar and melted chocolate until smooth.

Warm the rum until fizzing round the edges.   Remove from the heat and stir in the drained gelatine. Mix until smooth.

Pour the rum mixture in to the chocolate mixture.   Stir well and pour in to pretty glasses or ramekins.   Chill in the fridge for 4 - 6 hours or overnight until set and ready to serve with cherries soaked in brandy or kirsch.

If you make them in ramekins you can turn them out by dipping the base quickly in to boiling water and running a sharp knife around the edge.

PASSION FRUIT TART

To serve 10 - 12

12 passion fruit to produce
9fl oz/250ml passion fruit pulp
10oz/275grms caster sugar
8 eggs
10fl oz/300ml double cream
1/4pt/150ml single cream

FOR THE PASTRY
9oz/250grms plain flour
6oz/175grms butter
1 beaten egg
a tablespoon of milk

Equipment a loose-bottomed 10in diameter flan tin

Preparation
Make the pastry by rubbing the butter in to the flour to form breadcrumbs, then stir in the beaten egg and the milk to form a smooth dough.   Wrap in greaseproof paper and put in to the fridge to relax for 20 minutes.
Pre-heat the oven to gas mark 6/200c/400f.
Cut the passion fruit in half, scoop out the pulp and seeds and pass through a sieve in to a bowl to produce the juice.

Method
Roll out the pastry on a floured board and line the buttered flan tin.   Prick the base all over with a fork and line with a sheet of greaseproof paper and baking beans.   Place in the oven and cook for about 10 minutes before lifting out of the oven and removing the paper and beans.   Return to the oven to crisp up the base for another 5 minutes.   Allow to cool.

Sweeten the fruit pulp with sugar.   Break the eggs in to a separate bowl and whisk in the double cream.   Now add the fruit pulp and pour in to the waiting tart base.

Bake for 35 - 40 minutes until just set.   Remove from the oven and allow to cool to room temperature before serving with fresh berries and cream.

PRUNE and ARMAGNAC FRANGIPANE

To serve 8

8oz/225grms shortcrust pastry

8oz/225grms pitted Agen soft prunes
7fl oz/200ml Earl Grey tea
3 tablespoons armagnac

6oz/175grms unsalted butter
6oz/175grms caster sugar
3 eggs
4oz/100grms self-raising flour
2oz/50grms ground almonds
a few drops almond essence
a tablespoon of flaked almonds

8oz/225grms icing sugar
lemon juice
water

Preparation
Pre-heat the oven to gas mark 6/200c/400f.   Heat the tea with the armagnac
and pour on to the prunes.   Leave to infuse for 3 to 4 hours. Roll out the
pastry and line a buttered 8inch diameter flan dish.   Trim the edges.   Prick
the base all over and line with greaseproof paper and baking beans.   Bake in
the oven for about 10 minutes before lifting out and removing the paper and
beans.   Return to the oven for 5 minutes more to crisp up the base.
Remove and allow to cool.

Method
Pre-heat the oven to gas mark 4/180c/350f.   Strain the juice from the prunes
and roughly chop them.   Spread them across the base of the pastry case.
Beat together the butter and sugar until pale and creamy.   Add the eggs one
by one alternating with spoonfuls of flour.   Fold in the rest of the flour,
ground almonds and almond essence and spread this mixture over the
prunes.   Sprinkle flaked almonds across the top and bake in the oven for
35 to 40 minutes until risen and firm to the touch.   Remove and allow to
cool.

Sift the icing sugar and mix with lemon juice and a little water before
spreading over the top of the Frangipane.   Serve warm with creme fraiche.

WINTER PUDDING

To serve 4-6

1.5lbs/675 grms cooking apples
6oz/150grms dried apricots
6oz/150grms sultanas
7oz/175grms demerara sugar
6oz/150grms brown breadcrumbs
4oz/100grms unsalted butter
3/4pt/450ml extra thick double cream
2 glasses of water
the juice of a lemon
1 teaspoon ground cinnamon
a shot of brandy or calvados

Preparation
Peel, core and chop the apples. Chop the apricots. Take a heavy based pan
and tip in the apples, apricots, sultanas and cinnamon. Stir in
4oz/100grms of the sugar. Add the calvados, lemon juice and water and
stew uncovered until soft but not coloured. Set aside to cool.
Take a heavy based frying pan and melt the butter. Tip in the breadcrumbs
and cook, shaking from time to time, until crisp. Only then stir in the
remaining sugar and cook for a minute or two longer.

Assembly
The idea is to layer the fruit and breadcrumbs into pretty glasses finishing off
with a dollop of thick cream. Chill them until you are ready to serve and add
a shot of calvados before you finish off with the cream.

Cover photograph by Nigel Mackenzie